Whiskey

The story of the little pony that could.

written and illustrated by C.R. Arioto

This book is dedicated to my family:
My late father, Punky, my mother, Susan, and my two younger brothers, Riley and Garth.
We were fortunate to have lived in such an amazing place.
Many happy memories were made in
Pinehurst, California,
a little town within the Sequoia National Forest.

My love of horses started early, when I was just three.

Sitting astride my toy pony, giggling with glee.

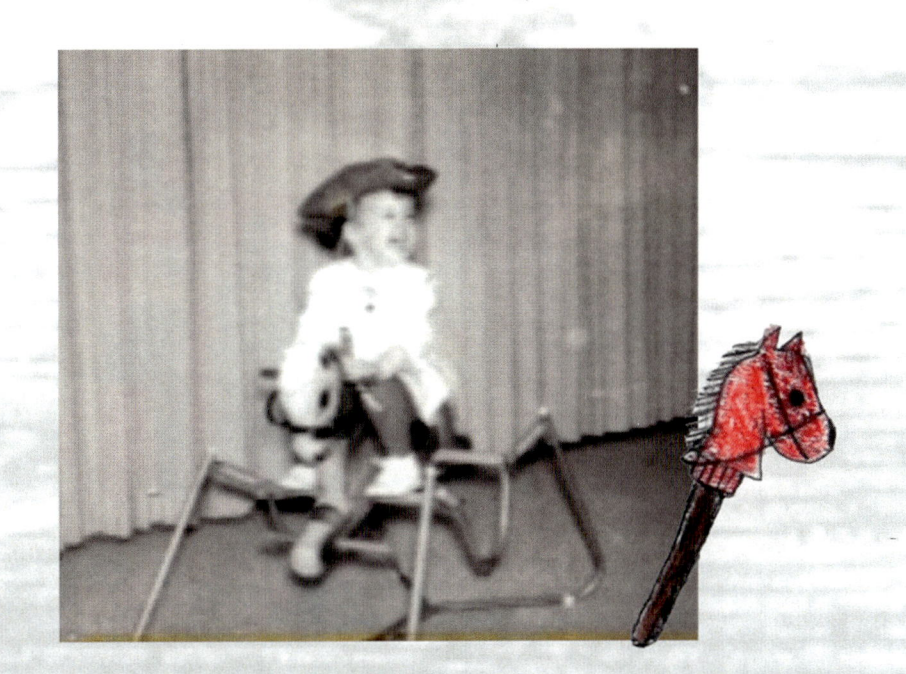

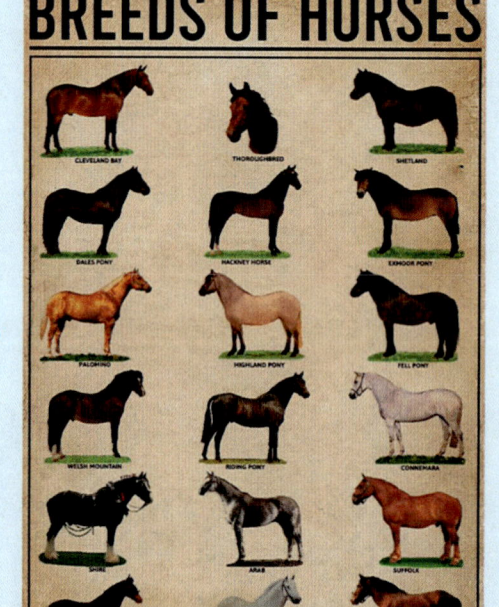

As I got older, I memorized breeds and knew them by heart.

I knew every fact and detail that set each one apart.

I drew horses by day, until
I made them right,

I read books about them
deep into the night.

I collected model horses in all shapes and sizes,

Placing them carefully on a shelf with my special prizes.

When I was 10, we moved to a place far away,

To a mountainous area with plenty of space to run and to play.

My love for horses never has wavered,

11

I would do anything to ride one,
including hard labor.

One day we went to a horse auction and sale,

My dream was true,
and not a fairytale.

There was this little pony that I really liked,

We bonded quite quickly,
I knew it was right.

His coat was brown and dappled, with a blonde mane and tail,

He had soft brown eyes that I trusted without fail.

He had on his face a white star and a blaze,

Making him look dashingly handsome in so many ways.

He had a thick neck and his legs had 4 socks that were white.

He had a big personality despite his small stature and limited height.

It surely seemed to be a match made in heaven.

Especially for a horse-crazy girl of eleven.

Whiskey Boy we named him and it suited him well.

He was no average pony;
he had the ability to fortell.

One day we were walking down a long winding road,

say what?

When Whiskey refused to keep going, despite being told.

I noticed some movement from the corner of my eyes,

It was a three-foot long rattlesnake slithering by.

He was the kind of pony that had lots of soul,

The type that would race bigger horses down a steep knoll.

We would go out for hours wandering along Cedar Creek.

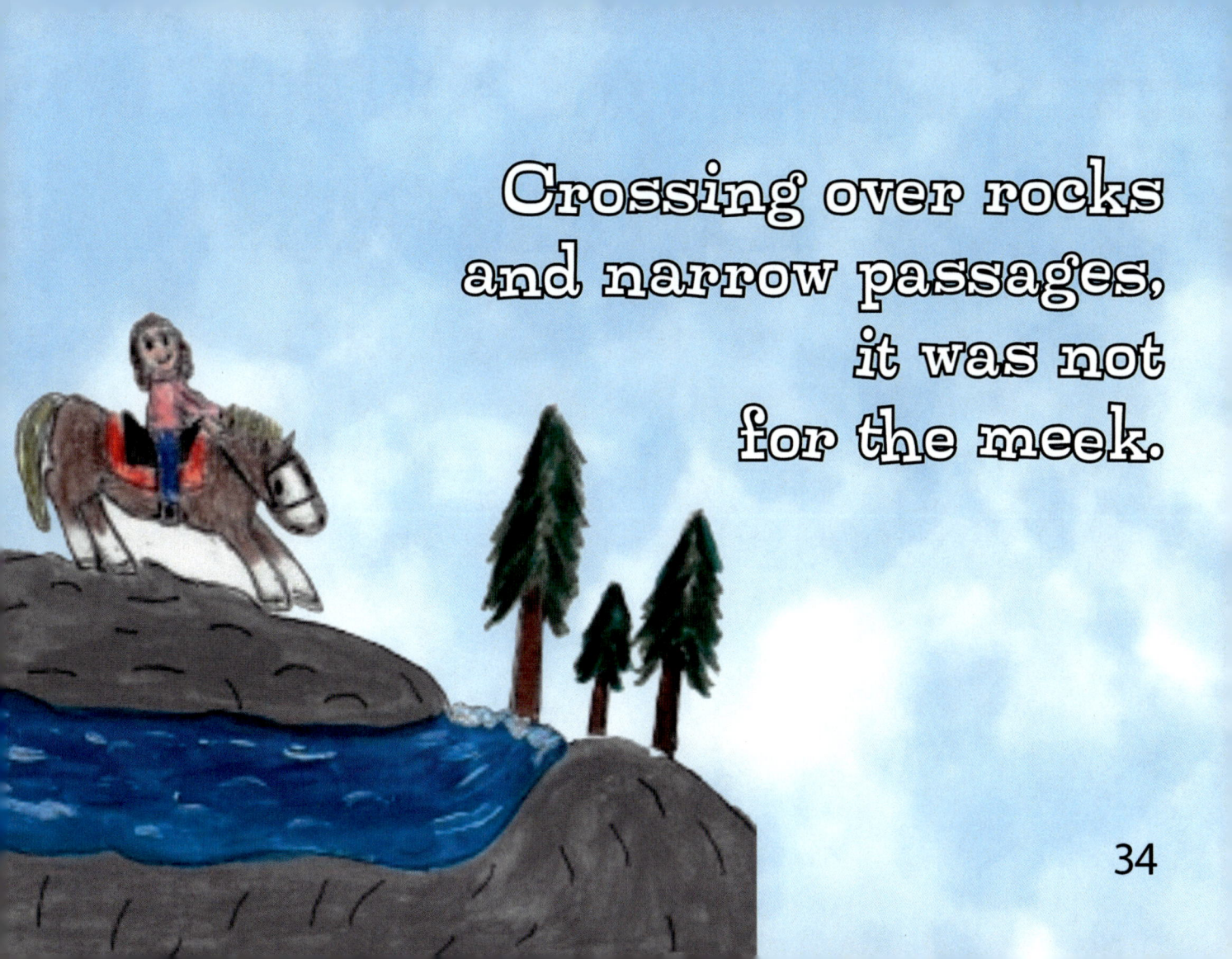

Crossing over rocks and narrow passages, it was not for the meek.

At the end of the day he would deserve a good treat,

Watermelon rinds were his favorite snack to eat.

If a young child
was placed on his back
for a ride,

Whiskey would take smaller steps and shorten his stride.

We would go out to the pasture to pick berries for a pie,

Only to find Whiskey's
head in the bucket,
eating our berries on the sly!

There was a horseshow planned in a town nearby,

Whiskey Boy and I decided to give it a try.

We practiced and practiced until
we got pretty fast,

We were ready, and the jitters became a thing of the past.

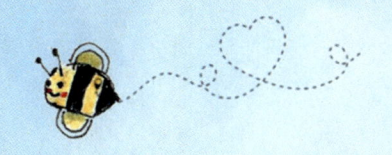

We had to walk five miles to the horseshow and back,

But we left as winners, with two firsts, two seconds, and a third to be exact.

I will never forget being so tired...

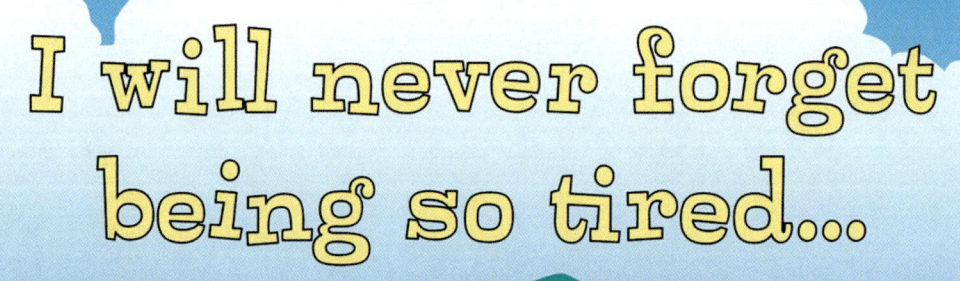

But it was Whiskey that deserved to be honored and admired.

He was the definition of spirit, tenacity, bravery, and good.

super pony

He will always be remembered as the little pony that could.

I think I can! I think I can!

The End

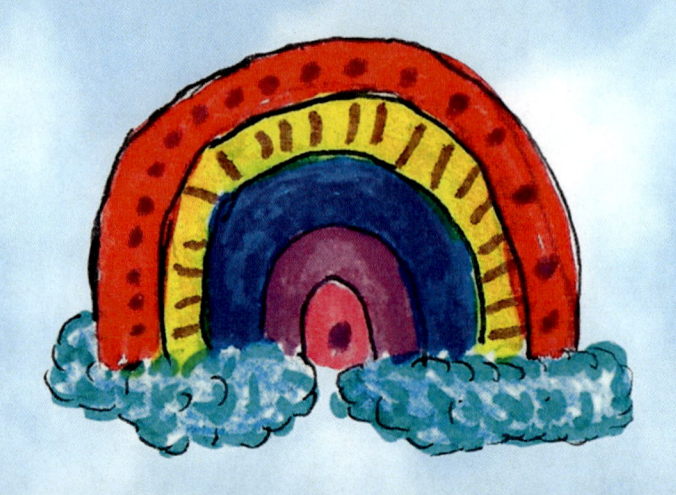

Notes from the author.

- Pinehurst, California is a real place. It is in the Sequoia National Forest, nearby is the Sequoia National Park, home of the infamous Giant Sequoias including the General Grant Tree.
- Pinehurst sits at 4200 feet elevation, population 595. It is located in the Sierra Nevada mountain range that creates the Central Valley of California to the east.
- It has a US Forest Service Ranger Station with fire services there. It is still in operation today.
- The nearest large town is Fresno, 60 miles away.
- Whiskey Boy was a Welsh Pony cross.
- Welsh ponies average between 13h and 14h. Whiskey as 12.2 h, suggesting he was a Shetland/Welsh cross.
- The Welsh pony makes a good starter horse for children due to their calm dispositions, yet can be challenging for more experienced riders.
- Welsh ponies are known for their versatility. They make excellent hunter-jumpers, and are often found in the show ring.
- They come from Wales where they were bred to be used in the mines.
- Many countries have their own breed of horses or ponies. In Ireland they have the Connemara pony and Gypsy Vanner also known as Cobb. Scotland has the Shetland pony, and the US has the Chincoteague pony, and Quarter pony. Germany has the Dulman pony, and England has the Dales pony.
- In the book I refer to reading books about horses. My favorite author was Marguarite Henry. She wrote many books about horses that filled my soul with amazement and wonder about these beautiful creatures. I read every single one of her books, and who knows, I may go back and read them again.
- My favorite horse books include: Anything by Marguarite Henry, especially <u>Misty of Chincoteague</u>, <u>Stormy Misty's Foal</u>, <u>Seastar, Orphan of Chincoteague</u>, and <u>Brighty of the Grand Canyon</u>.
- I also enjoyed <u>Black Beauty</u>, by Anna Sewell, and <u>Flicka</u> by Mary O'Hara.
- Happy reading.

Blue Bird Books
Ventura, California

www.bluebird-books.com

Made in the USA
Middletown, DE
03 November 2024